Praise for
Trees of Life and Shade

"Ron Searls, in his art as in his life, bridges the gulf C. P. Snow warned of between the culture of science and of literature. The subjects he takes on in his capable sonnets, odes, and elegies include astronomy, the Internet, flowers and trees, Greek mythology, human nature, and personal relationships and losses. He writes equally well about all these and more, and in doing so exhibits the craft of a mature poet. Most moving are the odes for his wife in her battle with cancer, his father's with Alzheimer's, and an elegy for a friend who died from AIDS."
––MARK PAWLAK, AUTHOR OF *RECONNAISSANCE, NEW AND SELECTED POEMS*

"Not a book to race through but rather one to savor, Ron Searls' *Trees of Life and Shade* includes both formal and free verse poems about trees, yes, but also poems about the Internet, volcanoes, cancer and T-cell counts, a Chinese pillow, Chopin, a dreaming cello, a puppet like a poem, myth, indeed the whole wild cosmos spinning with ants and termites to stars and planets. The collection is music in both subject and sound. The poems offer delights about what language can do with words combining and shape-shifting in provocative ways—'encrypted light,' 'dappled gloaming,' and 'gossiping leaves.' Thoughts launch the reader towards new contemplations—'If the end is beauty, to beauty we must evolve' and 'The fire of omniscience burned down to coals.' Sharp juxtapositions juggle one's sense of scale—'Holographic cities pulse on the skins of brown onions.' I think of Baudelaire or maybe Walt Whitman on a cosmic scale."
-ELIZABETH BODIEN, AUTHOR OF *BLOOD, METAL, FIBER, ROCK* AND *OBLIQUE MUSIC: A BOOK OF HOURS*

"*Trees of Life and Shade* travels life and the world, exterior and interior, the charted and the too often uncharted. As few others are, these poems are intent on the recovery from past concealments of self—encounters which bring us face to face with the full wonders he's coaxed from nocturnes, seasons, aubades, laments, exotic cafes, Mnemosyne, herself, cancer and even the internet. In doing this, he's opened himself to the ideas of desire, mortality, beauty and memory—the pursuit of the necessary—the revelation of the true self, giving voice to us."

–G. E. Schwartz, author of *Only Others Are, World,* and *Thinking in Tongues*

"Ron Searls offers up dexterous juxtapositions of sound and meaning. The poems portray sensitivity to the natural world and its cycles, to the vastness of the universe and its enigmatic parts—and the ways in which these wonders interact with human existence in all its shades. In Searls' vision the convergence of the metaphysical with the materiality of the everyday produces striking results."

–Laura Johanna Braverman, author of *Salt Water*

"Searls moves us through time, isolated moment by isolated moment. He lifts us from a garden's dirt and gives us eyes that see life through the leaves—the birth of everything—over a volcanic edge into the great unknown. He guides us through history, looking down at an artist thumbing the clay of words, the longing of a lost cello, the lost rulers and old gods. He brings us the embrace of the moments just before tragedy, with language that leans wide but true around the first and final bend of living."

–Robin Sinclair, author of *Letters To My Lover From Behind Asylum Walls*

TREES

OF LIFE AND SHADE

TREES

OF LIFE AND SHADE

RON SEARLS

ROCHESTER, NY

Copyright © 2019 by Ron Searls. All rights reserved.
Published by Cosmographia Books, Rochester, NY

No part of this publication may be reproduced, distributed, or transmitted in any form or by any means, including photocopying, recording, or other electronic or mechanical methods, without the prior written permission of the publisher, except in the case of brief quotations embodied in critical reviews and certain other noncommercial uses permitted by copyright law.

Cover and book design by Nina Alvarez
Cover photo by Ron Searls

For permission to reprint portions of this book, or to order a review copy, contact editor@cosmographiabooks.com

ISBN-13: 978-1-7322690-7-1

Contents

The Trees of Life	11
To a Glass Mercury	13
Ode to the Internet	15
The God of Stoned	18
Meditations on Chopin's Nocturnes	20
Mauna Kea	22
Enceladus	23
The Chinese Pillow	26
Wild Things	31
Garden Sonata	32
The Sea	37
The Death of Leviathan	38
Summer's End	44
Euterpe	47
The Dreaming Cello	48
On Poetry	49
Cappella Palatina	51
In the Tombs	53
Willow	55
Songbird	56
The Unmerged Star	57
Lethe	58
Lament	60
Aubade	62
To Devin	63
The Puppet	64
Evening Song	65
Sometimes I Wake	66
Evening Sonnet	68
The Empty Room	69
On Her Cancer	71
Bonebreaker	74
The Winter of Life	76

Autumn Interrupted	78
A German Requiem (1968)	80
Café Budapest	86
Half Life	89
Le Tombeau de Faisal	93
Elegy for John B_____	94
Mnemosyne	98
Rite	100
Midnight Sonnet	102

For my dear friend of over fifty years,
Saud Al-Sowayel. Classmate,
poet, translator, patron,
abiding inspiration.

For my beloved wife, Lore Nielsen,
high school crush whom I courted
for fifteen years, lost twice, and
finally won. Lover, friend, mother of
my children, PhD, survivor, muse.

The Trees of Life

The trees again in sync are singing
In their winter voices' twelve-tone scale.
They sing the leaves of summer fading
The riots of shades of leaves in fall.
They sing the hawk that through them hunting
Leaped sudden from meadow at the sky.
They sing the storms of ice arriving
That will crack the trunk and break the limb.
They sing the ones among them swaying
That will fall to oblivion below their feet.
They sing in their resonant choirs moaning
Of the eternal returns of freeze and heat.

And when the icy full moon's brightening,
Things of the future they see up high,
As their branches in the winds are waving
In cyclic eruptions of encrypted light.
They sing of what will be, transpiring,
The new that rises, the old that falls,
Ethereal notes from tomorrow migrating,
Soft oracles uttered to the dark,
Then fluttering low and triple tumbling,
Lost children scrying for a crumb,
Seeking the present in dappled gloaming,
Murmuring motets of things to come.

Trees of Life and Shade

The wind is the forest's scyther reaping:
The doom of everything is to fall.
Behind our house an oak was swaying,
Raging at a nor'easter's gale.
All night he sang full throated, wailing,
Defying the cutting ice and snow,
All night he sang full throated, failing
At last in gray and grim twilight,
Covered in winter before collapsing
To the abyssal wooden, rooted dun,
In the dying night now himself dying,
Revealed in the morning's frozen sun.

But summer returned, its warmth transforming,
New things to the oak corpse came:
Bark beetles first, then borers tunneling
Through sapwood and heartwood, then the queens
Of ant and termite, while outside hanging
Came mosses, lichens, algae, ferns
And fungi into mushrooms fruiting—
A fairy forest for spider webs—
Where ladybugs cluster in winter warming
And salamanders hide from strife.
Though wind and winter do their killing
The silenced become the trees of life.

To a Glass Mercury

You orbit a desk, cached in a lucid sphere,
With burnt red dark-side, craters done in swirls,
With sun-side white with light green crystals pearled,
A model of a planet suspended in slow glass.
What motioning hand from silica formed you?
Who drew you molten, into a globe within a globe?
Wandering star that naked eye can see
Already in Sumer, then south of Babylon
Of lapis lazuli your ziggurat to heaven rose.
Enki, Nabu, Coyote, Pusan, Thoth,
Budha, Hermes, Apollo, the Water Star,
Have you been called, trickster, wise one, thief,
Quickener, lyre giver, herald of the gods.
The eye of Galileo traced your paths,
Schiaparelli caught you stopped within his lens,
Copernicus, Kepler, Newton your orbits drew,
Upon which Einstein could precession plot
That we might calculate for Mariner an arc
Round Venus for an improbable carom shot
To toss cross vacuums that true face to us
That I now gaze on within this glassine ball.

We have unfixed the stars, the universe
Now's thrown apart, nomads are we all
Of the infinite vacant dark. Yet here you rest,

Trees of Life and Shade

Traveler from dream, to truth, from truth to art,
Contained and unperturbed, reminding us
That only change is changeless, and this resolve:
If the end is beauty, to beauty we must evolve.

Ode to the Internet

Give me one mouse, one keyboard, one hi-res screen
With diodes built of rainbows, an ISP,
And I will vault in instants time and space,
Cross chasms of logic, leap death's interface,
Like Mercury from Olympus plunge
To an electric earth on wings of silicon.
Mt. Fuji I'll graze in fuzzy view—speed
Through traffic jammed in Singapore, watch
White sands drift on Bahrain's empty streets,
While London sleeps and cocktails wet the lips
Of strapless furies perched on Harvard's bridge.

With amplified ears the whispers of the world
I'll hear: the gossips, rumors and the shouts,
The world wide mob, like Babel's chanticleer,
Trumpeting dawn at every hour: nostrums,
Potions, tidbits, cures, lies, deceits
And self-delusions dressed in purple gowns
Of truth. In sudden symposia in the night,
With pure intellects will I carouse and chase
Bold insight as it raptors down, towards strange
Attractors in a fractal scene, aching to disclose
In theories of the quantum, everything.

All libraries, all books, I will rework
Into ethereal pages, scripts of light

From which I'll weave, with knots of links, a cloth
Of lucent silk, embroidered with Homer, tales
Of Rome, Arthur, Dante and the Bard,
Bright stars set over wide fields of bones,
Torture and wrack and every fetid thought
Escaped from dark alleys of the slithering soul
Until—drunken with making, I lay down
My head upon the keys of this machine,
And sleep, the creature of a new, a digital muse.

In whiteout dreams she calls, she calls to me;
With hair of twisted cable-fire bright
She beckons—writhes—in pixels of flesh-tones
And blind blue eyes; glossed lips she presses close.
In her cold arms I've languished, like Rhymer's ghost,
While the world turned, as she did feed me fruit
From Eden's sinful tree, that I am become
Adam bestowing names, or the Alchemist
With the philosopher's stone, or Magellan,
More than once each day, encroaching
Whirling globes that sextant's never known.

But not to awake to godhead. The price is this:
A spotted hand, curled talon-stiff around
A pencil, scribbling words, things of the past,
Mere ciphers of what once was in this reach,
The fire of omniscience burned down to coals;
And that which Lucifer felt, as he looked back
Upon all the glory from that he fell,
Now in its fullness grasped, because apart;

And desire unslaked, which like a drug can rack
The ever questing mind, in its wired cell,
Till recursion halt the heartbeats of the heart.

The God of Stoned

In green palaces of exultant jade, whipped into swirls
Of frenzy, languorous texts slide, slithering in sheets
Of broadsides, words twisting, writhing into scripts
More serpentine than caducei, which tease of
Poetry sensed, not understood, while canopic jars
With galaxies full, momently tumble, to be replaced
By universes that were never born, but oh, will come,
In the domain of the kingdom of the God of Stoned.

The walls like garlic taste and spiced green oranges,
Holographic cities pulse on the skins of brown onions
Peeling away, one after one, then one, with towers
Of wonder between which angels fly under alien suns
And ringed planets and stippled moons and in their eyes
Are tunnels, hotlines into other times and spinning worlds
Where beings dream of beings dreaming dreams of him
Who is lost in the banquet hall of the God of Stoned.

The music of creation seeps from every implement,
Screwdrivers and hammers sing and the torque wrench
Chorus descants the scores of an unseen Tallis, while
Organ pipes scream with cartoon mouths puissant
From every living pore, rainbows of sound coruscate
Out of purple yews and trees waver without a wind
Outside the pixelating stone, through melting glass,
Beneath the choirs of the cathedral of the God of Stoned.

No brain can fix upon the inconstant fly, or its bred
Algorithms find pattern in the pearl, motion is all
In the red-rimmed cloisters that once were rooms,
Whose doors open onto craters on unknown moons
Which now are filled with blue flowers, gigantic gems
And strange machines which speak in a mathematics
That when unencrypted lead to other-grained realities,
As history evolves in the museum of the God of Stoned.

Aztec ziggurats against an azure sky, in steps rise up,
As dripping hearts bounce down like ping-pong balls,
Painting crimson ruin beneath the web of azimuths
Like a Pollock driven mad by the *res publica* of death,
While a solo arm in flash-stopped motion upraises
The scalpel stone, sharp, shedding lightning forks of fate,
As this one inescapable moment completes the path:
You are the sacrifice on the altar of the God of Stoned.

But lost—now the infinite vacuum: emptiness,
Ashes of bones, ashes of stars, red dwarfs as warm as ice
And only black holes, the gatherers of dust, detritus
And the wrecks of all that was, emptying the emptiness
Of the ever ballooning dark, as Gabriel's quantum horn
Is stretched to an impossible bass which throbs so low
It nausea becomes, the soul sick with a longing as deep
As the terrible beauty of the Tantalus God of Stoned.

Meditations on Chopin's Nocturnes

Fingers at a keyboard, like dolphins poised in glide,
To dive—hunt—streak—through swells of chords,
Clefs, flats and sequences in a minor key . . .
The dead hand's moved, its notes transcribed and ruled,
Sublimed into a pattern, cloned, and cloned again:
We copy to survive. And another dead
Pianist reliquefies the pattern, Rubinstein,
Transmuted by a microphone, mastered
On a platter, stored, and copied yet again
And now inscribed as dots, by laser light
From microscopic lands reflected, read,
Then changed to electrons, then to sibilant air,
Then to my ear, my brain, and now my heart.

Is it Chopin that I hear? Or do I merely parse
An electric muse from an electric sea?
Or is it more? I cannot bear to listen, I cannot bear
To have a weight, to be embodied when
I want to be a thing of pure frequency, a sonic
Attitude. It is I who am being played,
I am the thing transmuted. But a pattern's all it is,
Air moved quickly for a time and stopped.
Music's an algorithm, a recipe, a clock.
How can it touch and instrument my soul,
Play me like an organ with pipes and stops?

Words cannot bear this weight and crack . . .
Chopin, you dear,
Candlelight in winter
The sky before the dawn
The last stars fading
The kisses for hours gone
The world alone
Champagne in silver
The languor after love
Hours without sleep
And a cool breeze

Nothing is adequate
The world must be reformed
Your music its physics
Your transitions its logic
Your notes its words
What poetry that world
Would make . . .

Mauna Kea

I stood at world's edge, on red raw earth,
Above rafts of clouds kindled by the sun
And saw with prism shattered eyes the birth
Of all creation. Quasars had then begun
To shine like watchfires across all space,
While galaxies, like lovers in strife,
Embraced and parted, planets set in place
To become the cradles of incipient life.
With a million eyes with star dust lined
The universe is an enigmatic friend,
If one signal, one sign, one pattern we can find
In its dusk face, all loneliness will end,
And there will come a supernova so bright
That it will forever annihilate the night.

Enceladus

Can I sing of impossibility?
Imagine: you stand on Enceladus
On a crazy cracked folly of ice
Stiffer than granite
Reflecting white diamonds
Watching ice waterfalls fall up
You could think lashes, combs, feathers
Or the hair of a white witch
Wind tunneled at supersonic speed
Trailing to the stars

But hundreds of miles high?
Think rockets launching
Second upon second
Or fireworks on a lunatic scale
Or mad rainbows
In space kaleidoscoping
While your neck bent
Back into a right angle
You scan the black invaded sky

And look to your right
A face of fire
As close as death
Titanic Saturn looms

Scythed in half by the edge on rings
Bearded in ring shadows
Its storms blink out time
As you walk in its planet-light
The color of champagne

But think, the ice is
Water breathed out
From the ocean
Underneath the frozen rind
And in that occulted sea
In a living dark
Longing to be known
Revelation waits

We are in the darkness
In the blackest bowers of space
Looking at a door
Edges bleeding light,
The glow of another universe
Where every star is
A burning hearth

O moon of dreams
If you are pregnant
If your ocean is the amnion
Of other forms evolved
Then what you birth
To our wide eyes
Are waterfalls of ultraviolet flowers

That dance in the rise
And fall of binary suns
And sprays of purple tigers
Stalking prey in a red dwarf's rays
And birds that soar forever
In the shifting glow of sister moons
And rockets of intellects actinic
That a poetry of alien beauty
In calligraphies of blue starlight
In countless otherworldly visions
Broadcast across the infinite night

O universe of endless life
No longer alone
It calls to us

O Enceladus

The Chinese Pillow

In *The New York Review of Books*
I read about China's golden age—
By a muse of paper and ink inspired
I wrote these words upon a page:

"In the time of the Tang, the Emperor Ming
Bid his armies the sunset desert wrest
And the way unblocked to Samarkand,
He craved the glamour of the utter west."

"A plant of darkness, a wind emitting stone,
A pot that cooked without a flame,
Red wheat that let its bearer fly,
On dromedaries down the Silk Road came."

"A pillow of crystal, most rare of all,
To those whose heads upon it lay,
Gave visions of alien worlds and strange,
As they dreamed a moonlit night away."

But was there really such a thing?
Could I sleep on a pillow carved from stone?
For days and nights I searched the Web,
For auctions of Chinese things to own.

Then I found a pillow of forest-green jade,
With calligraphy snaked like a stream,
That spelled a work of the poet Li Po:
"Tianmu Mountain Ascended in a Dream."

A half-poetic moonshot this—
I wrapped it in a woven spread
And slowly placed my shuttering eyes
On this makeshift version of a bed.

And dreamed of worlds where time grows old,
Where pale moons race in purple skies
And cleaved minds sip from fluted flowers
And make love where the cool grass lies.

I dreamed of beings with blood like wine,
In a city that spanned a million stars,
Who, drunk on music and poetry,
Tattooed whole planets with rifts like scars.

I met beings colder than fire ice
That sipped on intergalactic light
And drifted in dark matter clouds
As they plotted a single atom's flight.

I saw stars of diamond in rosettes arranged
By a race of vanished engineers—
Night's jewelry on a cosmic scale
That will sparkle for ten billion years.

Trees of Life and Shade

I dreamed of worlds in water globed
Where whale songs reverb'd planet-wide,
And ten thousand-mile waves forever flowed
On a sister planet's tugging tide.

I saw beyond number red dwarfs dim
With planets warmed by the infrared,
Where even in dark russet light
Black flowers grew and slow things bred.

I saw colliding swarms of Milky Ways
Coalesce—seduced by gravity's desire—
Then suns cooking hydrogen into gold
And quasars setting galaxies on fire.

And I saw to the death of the universe,
As the last of life nursed the failing light,
And sang all creation's song again
In the final compline's lost midnight.

*   *   *

I awoke with a start, in the nesting dawn,
To recall what in the dark took wing,
And put the jade pillow on a shelf:
It was, at the end, just a beautiful thing.

A cup of coffee, a piece of toast,
Thus dawn does dreaming reimburse—
And though of this earth I must remain,
I sing to the rocket of my multiverse.

It's this wet machine, the brain evolved,
In this one moment, in this single place,
That throughout all of time can trawl
And till the quantum fields of space.

O take me to a star and back,
Then take me on to Saturn's rings,
Fly me through the molten sun,
Let me hear the songs the vacuum sings.

Let me cross uncountable galaxies
On wormholes that make a paved highway,
Let me fall into an old black hole—
Live a million years as if a day.

And when heart slows as all hearts must
And when bone breaks and ears lose sound
I will need no pillow for my greying head
As this body crumbles to the ground.

AUTHOR'S NOTES:

I first read about the crystal pillow and the other magical things mentioned in quatrains two through four in an article in the *New York Review of Books*, "China's Golden Age" by Eliot Weinberger, published November 6, 2008:

> *The masses, who rarely saw these treasures, told tales of strange objects with magical powers, brought from abroad: a single bean that was sufficient food for weeks; a certain wheat that made the body so light that one could fly; a crystal pillow that gave the sleeper visions of strange lands; a piece of rhinoceros horn that could heat a palace; hairpins that turned into dragons; pots that cooked without fire; the translucent stone that emitted a cool breeze; the plant that was always surrounded by darkness.*

Emperor Ming is the Tang Emperor Xuanzong. The poem 'Tianmu Mountain Ascended in a Dream' is by the Tang poet Li Bai. English translation by Witter Bynner. "Li Po" is an older way of referring to Li Bai.

Wild Things

On Thanksgiving, thirty or so turkeys
Motored into the yard on clawed wheels
Like Brando and the wild ones.
They are indifferent, intent on earthworms,
But, as if warned by invisible sentinels,
They slide away when I sidle close.
They are familiar and disdained,
Yet evolve in a parallel world,
Intertwined with and dark to our own.
Without language, who is to say
That they do not calculate or feel?

I love wild things. They live
Beautifully in the enigma of the other.
They temper the loneliness
That anticipates the dark.
They roost in the beguiling woods.
They bring their children
Into our gardens.
In winter, when leaves
Are burned away, they look up
And do not see the stars we do,
But something alien, lovely and bright.

Garden Sonata

—propter amorem amicorum

I

In my garden late, summer often holds its breath,
Its gossiping leaves stopped listless in suspense,
And a stillness falls, as if down comes death
Like a red-tailed hawk, and all is silent, tense.
The mower next door shuts up its bladed howl,
And eighteen wheelers' tires no longer scream,
The jets above fly off and with their growl—
Not one made thing dares decibels redeem.
I sink into this quiet, quiet zone
And hear what now I never heard before:
The fountaining fall of water on stone—
The catbird launching from the mulch strewn floor.
To the columbines twists the hummingbird:
Fro to, down up, vectoring the nectar near,
Then rubied throat sweet sipping—half heard
Its manic wings, so swift is their career.
It's all primeval, in this stippled plot,
The stones coalesced billions of years ago,
Cooked from a violent supernova's clot
In titanic collisions caught in gravity's throw.
And on this stone the trilling waters run
With that same tone that no ear heard
When first our ripening earth, under pulsing sun,

Lay naked, glistening, waiting to be stirred.
But then long time—time then longer still—
Before the ancient archaea swarmed into the boil
Of molten geysers, and here their offspring fill
The rooted loam, the green sustaining soil.
The goldfish glinting in the pond, are cousin to those
Same pisceans that in primordial seas, when all
About was desert, from land ablated pools arose
To gasp on air, on spiny fins to crawl.
Dusky mosses the paving tiles outline;
They sip on moisture, mate by wandering winds,
For a hundred billion days sun-rays refine,
By simplicity escaping all cataclysmic ends.
The younger ones, viburnum, meadowsweet,
For billions of days have thrived and their sweet flowers,
And all their insect acolytes so fleet,
Trading nectar for pollen, in endless golden hours.
And as the evening falls, in twilights long,
The bats, born after flowers and the dinosaur,
Their dreams contrive in ultrasonic song,
Before the moon: arc, arc, and arc and soar.

II

What of the garden of the greater world, of which
My own's a softscaped nook? The climate heats,
As if a fire-mouthed dragon stalks the rich
Ecosphere of our one home, excretes
Hot breaths across the glacial ice and snows,

With planet spanning soughs warms up the poles,
Against rain forests gutting red flame throws,
And microwaves across the permafrost rolls.
Its wings spin up wild wailing hurricanes,
Tornados and cyclones ride its twirling claws,
Deserts and droughts it leaves as its remains,
Its watch is sleepless, pitiless, without pause.
This runaway feedback monster, so sly and slow,
Will lead us in a fuming totentanz
Spinning us into dervish a-go-go
Till the dancer is disintegrated by the dance.
Will we like Venus end wrapped up in shrouds
Of metal slagging heat, the world beneath
A barren cook pot steaming endless clouds,
A pressurescape grinding volcanic teeth?
And is that great silence, when we outward gaze
And ask the stars for signs of other life,
Because no other planet beyond itself could raise
Its eyes to heaven without world consuming strife?
It is the age Anthropocene; we dominate,
Selection by nature become selection by man.
Will we be the equilibrium of nature's fate?
Or the *modus tollens* that extinction began?
Small purpose through patient evolution flowed,
From this machine conscious minds emerged,
Until we youngest stood, to see the rose as rose,
And life itself, into self awareness surged.
We are creation's eyes, but that same gift
Makes us to us absurd. Self-blinded, we think
That we from some far heaven fall and drift

Into the body, that we to mere existence sink.
We feast on lies, like black and querulous crows,
Bite out the eyes from the ravaged corpse of truth,
And murder to liberate, as if the throes
Of death were jaunts to neverlands dripping ruth.
We are the fire that burns, extinction's maul,
The sorcerer who into poisonous potions delves,
Ending genomes and species with profligate gall
And laying waste to nature, waste ourselves.

III

No creator will save us, if we drag earth to hell.
We crawled from the sea, stood up from mud,
Each generation we remake from one small cell
And from mere gradients create both bone and blood.
In months we build what evolution took
A trillion days to mold: the brain which brings
Us love and hate, the symphony, the poem, the book,
The psalm: there is a genius in the smallest things.
Creation creates itself, and should we fail
In our great uplift, earth will still abide
And that great cradle may new forms entail,
Life again upon a cooling earth may stride,
Or that large universe that fills the dark
With inevitable life may burst and roil and teem,
And with more wisdom on some other ark
Than ours, eyes may also look out and dream . . .
Do you hear it? Water still down gray stone

Runs, bees and wasps buzz riot in the leaves,
To my green chapel I return alone
And rest under maple and rhododendron eaves.
And when I think that there is less of life than more,
That that last evening will soon arrive for me,
I sit in my living cloisters as around me soar
The creatures of a summer, coptering in manic glee.
A thousand palettes of emerald glow, the sky
Soon deepens to electric blue, red flowers' perfume
Hallucinogenic wreathes, as summer whirls by
Like a maypole girl caught up in her own zoom.
But a moment's revelation too soon is past
And that same lack forces us to yearn.
It is more tender because it does not last—
There is no beauty without death—we learn.
Our art then renditions instants out of time
That we may have posies of the passing while,
It mutates transience into changeless rhyme
And the love we long for into Da Vincis of a smile.
So I will go when summer's last lights rue,
When twilights linger long at night's black door,
And in that glimmer with my arching mind review
What in the living universe has gone before.
The future awaits for more future eyes than ours,
And the beauty that will come—how it does call—
If we yet last to dwell in golden hours
And the universe itself itself enthrall.

The Sea

The sea shall return, waves of white horses
Galloping on green glass, and the creatures
Of the sea flying like cool machines, jetting
In bubbles and blood lust, in iridescence,
Which is no color, but the micro flashes
Of fallen suns, and the deeps of the sea
So dark and thick, where vents boil up
The broth which cooks new life.

And the men shall return, having sailed
On the Brownian sea, corpses spanking
The shore, crawling on the crying sand
Where crabs, like robots, gnash, scrabble,
Amid the detritus and seaweed which
Dances on the round rocks and hisses
At the snaking threads of watery
Rope, where driftwood yearns for fire.

There are those of the sea, and those
Which walk by it and lust for the difference
And the agony, which is not for them,
But they wonder what it would be
To be of the sea, to be lost in infinite
Space, in restless expanses, with
Islands like planets and voyages that end
Only at the stun of new worlds.

The Death of Leviathan

*Leviathan, the great whale, poet of whale song, loved the earth,
and her spirit, and sought her, his muse, in every place.*
–Author

Over the sunken argosies of Spain,
Where the treasuries of lost peoples
Spilled upon the sandy plains
Of boiling tropical seas and fretted shallows,
Roamed Leviathan;
He sang to the volcanic mounts,
The sinking moon, the million molten stars
Hung above the island clinging reefs,
Hymns to the cradles of brilliant fish,
To scintillant bright cephalopods amid
The forests of lazy kelp and frozen ferns,
Anemones, crustaceans and all
The watery creatures spawned
Across the billion pentads of her life,
She, the earth, for whom he longed.
Through the wrecks and columns
Of shaken marble, the jars of olive, jars of wine
And the fallen gods
Of Athens and of Rome
And the bleak warships of Persia
And those vanquished by Greek Fire
And the wiles of Archimedes,

Up to the edge of those timbered, scabrous hulks
That once bridged old Hellespont,
There breached Leviathan;
Then by vacant deserts and the Atlas sere,
Through her stone dressed thighs,
Into the stormy southern latitudes
And the myths of Atlantis
And her tawny African shore,
Circumnavigated he.

Long was his journey, always the journey,
Distant, distance to the ends drawn,
Scanning her many forms,
The volatile moods of her, then her
Utter stillness in the sea becalmed;
Drawn ever into her endlessness,
Restless, to the south he edged
Until the sun never set
On the ice, cracking in canticles.
And the cantos of glacial groans
And the song of the spalling surf,
All heard Leviathan in the cold and rime,
As the pendant cities of ice rose, momently
In the edging sun, with all colors imbued,
Krill, penguin, seal, walrus, orca
Mobbing the frozen island earths
Before they were effaced—
And all, in the abyss,
Was drowned.

Into the open, reckless Pacific
Where she bade cloud kingdoms rise
And reign and within a day to fall
Or blossom into cloud flowers
That kissed the vaulted stratosphere
Like pink hibiscus at every dawn,
There into the storms and cyclones
Which she stirred with idle fingers,
There Leviathan, below the surface, sailed
Against the precipices and long green shoulders
Of her side-glancing hills, with her fans of forests raised,
Shyly, hiding the brown eyes, as she bathed
Cascading. As it rose, her breath
And then his, as he crossed the thermoclines
And the giant twirling blue vortices
And the planet spanning currents
Of rivers within rivers and seas within seas
And all the boundless fecundity of the ocean-bride
Amid the spinning centricity of the silver schools,
To the north he sped, as if to a great attractor drawn
In the chaos of the wavefronts and clashing waves—
But under the riot of Borealis, by the Bering Sea,
There, as he heaved, repenting of breathless dives
And dreamed of rejoining the hidden wetness of her,
Great Leviathan fell.

Impaled, impaled, he dragged her weight—
For one long hour he turned the globe—
As boats leaked rusty wakes behind
And devil floats buoyed him up against

The temptation of the cool blue-green dive.
Long, long trolled he his fate behind him . . .
Until the cetacean heart of him failed . . .
Until all lust lay motionless . . .
Until the kill lance pierced,
The carnelian spume coughed,
And the yellow sun cooked unclosed eyes.

Red glories lay tattered then, tangles of flesh, flayed,
Red life reflected in the blades of the flensing,
The white giant now in relentless stages scathed:
Blanket slabs into horse pieces cut,
Into bible leaves of blubber sliced,
The try pots fed, spermaceti drained,
Then the bones and the scrimshaw teeth,
On which bored sailors scratched out pictographs
Of whaling barks and punctured whales
In squeamish blue webs of suspended death.

But where the amber-grey? Where the miracle?
The change of what is gone, the left-behind
The forgotten, into earth's seduction?
And where, where among that gore
The wanderer who loved, father of the song?

I am not the self:
I am the broken voice
That emerges from, flotsam
Swirling in seas of connections
Washed up upon that shore gleaming,

From which, after the comet fell,
In the womb of her, he evolved,
Answering her wailing call,
Back into the beckoning waves
Where chosen, sounds he, still
(We came too late)
That sound that cannot still.

He pings the infinite abyssal,
Diving through turquoise
Down cerulean
Down indigo, down
Down midnight, down
Down beyond her, down
Where the ancient kraken awaits
In deeps of cold calculation, elegant—
Is the duel of minds?
Or is it the hunger?
That darkness is terrible
The pressure
Weighing
Against the buoyant
But still the echo locates the prey
We cannot breathe
But there
Its lidless eye appraises, fleeing
But faster we
As the sweet flesh slides inward
But the raptor mouth inside us
Like the grit, the pearl

But up, up we must
Bursting, ache, arcing to breathe
Against the murderous air
And the treachery of the gray green sea
And the barbs of men
And the lethal pause—

O but then
But then to return

Above darks where earth's hot blood
Bubbled, pillowed up, screaming
And fumaroles who birthed hellish
Colonies of blinded beauty
Swam Leviathan;
Across lonely oceans over-cruised he
The detritus of war and gray iron
Graves with red coral overgrown,
Where white dead things dissolve,
Drowned in the mottled turrets,
Behemoths of anger,
In languorous green waves
And the huge black canyons where
Gigantic salten cataracts slide
In her secret grottoes
Far from the pallid eyes of men.

Summer's End

Long hours I've worked this stubborn clay of words,
And sought to throw, inscribed with subtle rhyme,
Cups in the kiln of language, therein to hold
The wines of inspiration and delight.
But my muse has fled, disdained these artful gifts,
With anger swept, with delicate wrist, them down
To shatter into shards of phrases, which
I shrift; and now, grown old, my hope remained
That I might find her yet in mundane things—
But while I pursued her, autumn came.

We went, in late September, to Fenway Park,
Where I watched the older boys of summer play.
Could I find her here, in greensward, lime and steel?
Was this stadium, cathedral, its players votive monks
With vestments, rituals and signs? Was this
Her passion play, retold each humid night
With anthems, victory or with sacrifice?
Or did she haunt the faces in the crowd
On skill intent, or the candied children
Giggling, plied with friends? Was it her voice
Serene, dispensing wisdom at my back,
Talking bunts, squeezes, balks and steals?
But before I beheld her, autumn came.

It came like Ares blitzing armies east,
Sky full of cannon thunder, barrel flash,
Skeening rain like bullets from heaven's gate,
And scattered the multitudes from their seats,
Bullied summer from her heated place,
Her kitchen and her parlor of hazy lace,
And sent us home. In the sudden chill
Of the next morning, it was time to pick
Apples and peaches, so we slowly drove
Through arched corridors of doomed green,
Where I noticed maples, like Judas, marked with gold,
And found her not, with summer she had flown,
For in the night time, autumn came.

In the orchard, with its rows of sorted trees,
Of Macs, of Empires, Cortland, Delicious red,
Small hands had plucked the lowest hanging fruit,
So I looked up—up to sky framed boughs,
And with superior height for ripeness searched.
My wife and daughter's voices faded then;
I forgot my duty to collect, as I scanned
High branches, paced from tree to tree,
Searching for perfection, sweet and modesty.
She must be there, in those studded choirs,
Where only I and the dragonfly could reach;
But though I strained to touch the reddest fruit
To sun exposed, each, when turned, was flawed
With green or bruises, and then it seemed that it
Was a metaphor of all my work, my life,
That I had gleaned. I bowed my head, abject,

Trees of Life and Shade

My ardor spent—then, on the ground, mottled
With dirt, I saw, in the intervening grass,
An unblemished apple—dropped there—where I
Hadn't cared to look. I buffed it with my shirt,
Kissed it, bit, as juices beaded on
A grizzled chin, heard laughter cool, fey,
Between the fretted shadows, almost a name,
And in its sweet remainder, autumn came.

Euterpe

She moved like hallucinated smoke,
In whorls of grace and firefly gleams.
Her earth colored eyes dissected hearts.
Her thoughts were hummingbirds in spring.

We lay in fields of lavender as summer
Glided above blue hills, her voice was water
Stretching over stone, and her touch
The wind that stirred the swaying stems.

She was all the ripe things of the fall,
The fullness of the grape, the gold of corn,
The harvest moon in sweeps of stars,
The music of wild geese winging home.

She was the fire that burns the heart,
The light that defies encroaching dark,
I loved her in four quarter time,
Till poetry sublimed like winter's frost.

The Dreaming Cello

You stand alone now, leaning on a chair
Waiting for the next embrace
Of artist, of lover,
A thing of wood, of maple, of spruce,
Taut strings and desire
From a luthier's mind—
Art to make art.

Baritone in a minor key
For centuries
Deepening adagios you have voiced,
You who are ageless made,
You outlive us, outlong us,
Who play you, who hear you,
And then, as we must, go on.

You will into beauty again awake
To draw the future the future to.
You're that eternity we can make:
For it's not the songs already sung
That compel us,
Though they be sweet,
But all of the songs to come.

On Poetry

Can you a poet be?
Surely you can put down words
And arrange them, rhyme them
(Or not, if you want to publish)
You can form them into forms
The sonnets, the villanelles
(Or not, if you want to publish)
But even if you write the words,
And see them into print
Can you a poet be?
And where there are great poems
Whose language is a fire
That burns out all the exaltation
In your heart
And you struggle to make your own
And fail
Can you a poet be?
But what if poetry is more than art
More than the words
So carefully arranged
What if it is the world itself
Which stuns you
In some small glance
Like irises shouting spring
Or when you look into the eyes

Of some wild thing
And both of you know you know
As you at its magnificence quail
Or when you walk
In the raw beauty of the
Complicated earth
And every inch of it
Is its own universe
Can you a poet be?
For it is not the words themselves
But that you have to recreate
—You must—
What was given unto you
And birth it into incandescent afterlife
In all the imagination of our kind
As that one holy duty—
You see
You cannot be a poet
—But must—
Let poetry be

Cappella Palatina

Transmuted into tessellations of gold
Reflecting myriads of restless flames,
A graphic novel floated above my head,
Its panels filled with stories that had flowed
From mouths to scrolls to codices,
In torrents of language, then to these walls,
A canvas hung a thousand years ago.
Captions in Latin explicated scenes
As the god of Genesis cooked up a world,
As Adam and Eve to mortality fled,
As Sodom exploded in red fire
And Abraham his kill knife raised,
And on and on, story on story,
Until my head was spun around
By epochal tales of the morning of Man
Inlaid in mosaics in the Byzantine style
With inscriptions and idle space filled in
With octagons, rosettes and swirling vines.
Then my eyes gyred higher still
To this chapel's stratosphere within,
Where it was not with the deity
And his warrior saints filled,
As you might want in this time of rage,
But with a *muqarnas* not even in Arabia seen,
Stalactites pendant in an amber sky,

Everywhere with pictures inscribed
Of falconry and lions and desertscapes,
Lords and ladies at the smallest scale,
A fractal, eightfold, symmetric dream
Carved by poets from the Maghreb.

Then I imagined another holy place
Not at all with images engraved
But with all the lines of poetry
From all the poets from all of time
That would fill the universe before my eyes
Wherever I cared to look—it was
The chapel of my mind I soon realized—
And then thought what it would be
To have been that imbricate mind
Which the Palermo chapel had conceived:
What wild arabesques that one must have seen,
What star-crossed tales beyond all reach,
What images, what tapestry,
What beauty swirling without form
Everywhere indwelling in all of space—
Then noticed once more—silent—still—
The remnant glass and stone and wood,
The shadows by creation cast—
Now lengthened beyond war and time
And limning transcendence—become sublime.

In the Tombs

You gods upon these dry demented walls,
Immense in the night, you in silence descend:
Down and down you come, in the deep tombs,
In the high tombs, glyphs become flesh, dropping,
You, fashioned with wild forms, half-animal, half-man.
Isis with your embosoming, encompassing wings,
You, Horus, raptor mouthed, black orbit eyes, watching,
And you, Anubis, preparer, your jackal-grin
As stiff as those you guide, and Thoth, ibis-beaked,
You wise one, your hand is poised to record each fate,
All of you wait, each night, in this court of Osiris,
Who wrapped in his gleaming linens, longs to induce
The newly judged into his otherworld.
All of you are surrounded by incantations, spells
To guide, and with the reliefs, of bountiful life,
Of hippos in lotus flowers, cow and crocodile,
Barley, bread and beer, of fishes in reefs,
Water-birds and snakes, and the great river,
To recall to life the souls of the dead. But where,
Where are the men? Where the women who dreamed you?
The mummies are gone. Robbed are the graves, vanished
The architects, painters, masons, carvers who shaped.
Scintillant universe, you called to us within
These shafts and branching deeps, these were your landings,
Obsidian the portals of immortality.

Only we, the last of men, slump by your walls
And with opaque eyes mere symbols see
Of eternal things, faded images on stone.
We occupy your days, in our shuttled crowds,
And leave, in our despair, to you only
The stillness of the everlasting night.
And here you remain, creatures of a million days,
Waiting and asking, asking that we decide:
If the poet leave, does the poetry abide?

Author's Note: The Ancient Egyptians believed that the subjects in the tomb paintings came alive after the deceased was interred.

Willow

O she is lissome, she is withy lithe,
Like smoke that curls and whorls in whirls—
Slow, slinky, unaccountably blithe
She about the world in winding twirls.
She is the spirit of the unfixed dream
That flows in beauty, point to surprised point,
The murmurations of starlings her thoughts seem,
As they turn and twist in glancing counterpoint.
She's entangled my heart in gossamer thread
As smooth as silk, as light as a spider's web,
That my heart's beats would surely shred—
But my thoughts on her yet wax, not ever ebb.
She is the moment that I cannot leave,
Fascination—lure—call—my Meave.

Author's Note: "Meave" is a variant of "Maeve."

Songbird

Acrobat of air, who could dive, arc and wheel
And utter cantatas in cathedrals of sky,
You are now imprisoned in filigrees of steel,
In a cell where alone, you will never more fly.
You belong in green jungles, a red tumbling grace,
Limb flung to limb, a flower taken wing,
A poet of free fall now confined to small space,
O Songbird, O Songbird why do you yet sing?
The music we make is the music that we hear
And far from the cacophony that braying life brings
Come distant strains to the solitary ear
And the spare pianissimo of eternal things.
My love, I willingly tender my art:
I'm the songbird encaged in the sonnet of your heart.

The Unmerged Star

This poet from his cometary drift
Was teased to life, lit like a latent star,
Whose feverish coalition was the gift
Of you, sun-muse, closing from afar.
You spun me up, my heart broke into fire,
And as our orbits, drawn together, sped,
We could not see beyond our flared desire:
To be was to be parted, joined, be dead.
Cooled white, to red, to black, in emptiness,
I have my self, but die the meaner death,
And you, my star-lost, waning in recess,
Are viewless, lost in heaven's frozen breath.
Bare words remain; they, like planets, fall
Around one shadow of a fond recall.

Lethe

She waits
In the backwaters of my soul
She swims
Beneath moss fall and cypress rise
She motions.

Her ice fingers reach into my heart
To chill the hot pulses of day,
Embalming the weary will.

She is there, among the late night yawns,
The twinging neck, the dewless eyes,
The sighs of eve's irresolution.

An empty mail box leads me on
Into her grotto—down—more blue than sleep,
More cold than Novocain,
Where her soft invitations underlie
The songs of others' loves.

Her touch is soothe and menthol on my back;
My muscles will not move again.
So easy it is to rest
In silences, in softness, in sighs;
Each breath is slow, then slower.

Barely the whisper,
The call upon my ear, "Come drink of Lethe:"
The death of love is love of death,
The death of love is death.

Lament

The chord, the song, is over;
Dionysus is gone;
Gone—the reeling dance of summer;
Gone—the melody a heart was born in.
Never again to sleep,
The soul;
Eyes cannot stop searching
For the unforgotten.

One was awakened;
Him, the stars, the sacred,
Cradling, glittering moon
Inspirited, outcalled in
Holy, the morning, the dawn
Of the promise
Is broken
The spirit, swollen tears, cold pain—
Ache, bone ache of the knowing—
Gone Dionysus—the god is gone.
In the wine sweetness, the white,
White, and white of the sun of the noon,
The other was loved;
In the living, the moment,
All
Is the one and peace

Heart quickening joy
Of Dionysus in the wine heat,
And the knowing to be,
And the god—
And the god is gone;
River running,
Sorrow unquenched
In the dry death of tears,
The heart torn, torn and bleeding
For want of the singing
Soul taking peace,
And the quiet, the absence,
The never, never, never
To touch, to be near—
The echo dying,
Chord fallen, my heart,
The song is over:
He is gone.

Aubade

The window grows transparent, love, our night
Must end. We made each other, in moonbeams, moan,
Our kisses knew not where or when, the sight
Of rendered flesh, our wetness, made us groan,
So in each other lost our couplings made
Of sensations: worlds:—spring, summer, fall
Revolved—fire—ice—heat—shade—
Brown earth was our twinned body, time our thrall.
We flow away, all flows away, on the flood
Of moments ferried—moon to sickle moon
We flower, then furl like autumn's faded bud.
But stay, the murmuring heart will quiet soon.
Love is not just the electric jangle height,
But the patient tender, even to that longer night.

To Devin

How—sweet boy—you lie,
Not yet shrouded in sleep,
But in a deeper peace:—life
Spirals out from thy
Softly hawk-edged fingertips;
Unseen, a majesty tangles thy hair.
So still—
Yet moves thy
Dreaming breath, in a rhythm
Stolen, in a rhythm kept,
That turned Copernicus with the stars.

The Puppet

Over here—a little—just—upon the shelf—
No—there—inside the box—that wooden thing
Of carven flesh, red cheeks, green felt,
Knobby elbows, a smile, though forced,
Which echoes what it often brings,
But now, a sad, limp puppet on jumbled strings.

To me, little hands once gave
These tangled guys, wires, twisted thread;
Beseeching from this crippled mess,
That I transform, into lines of grace;
And I, like some Leonardo of knots,
Angled my head, nodded, dipped—
Plotting courses, relations, functions, maps—
Swift to untwist, if not to bless—
And bundled my charges to their beds.

Deep was the silence of the thought:
There is no origami to this thread.
I cheat, then disassemble, to recreate;
I cannot undo what entropy has said:
I stand where once one master stood,
And dream, a simple poem, a thing of wood.

Evening Song

On the porch on that last night,
On the twilight of all twilights,
As the sun set, on the sunset of all sunsets,
As the world ebbed, all the world a raiment became
Of red and gold worked with life: swifts, swallows,
Robins, cardinals, screech owls, rabbits, oaks,
Maples, sycamores, beeches, cherries, peach—
And the susurrations of the breeze
And the tall grasses of summer.

And I loved you in that moment
And I loved you more in that moment
And I saw the world in your eyes and your eyes
Were the color of the world and your cheeks were
The ocher of the world and your lips were
All the lips that all lovers had ever kissed
Everywhere, in all time.

And we wore the world, full with its fullness,
Engorged with life and the fulfillment of things;
As the evening came, and the darkness,
And the fireflies in the darkness, we took
Off the world and folded it away and afterwards
Slept arm-in-arm, in the cool hours at midnight,
Wrapped in silent sheets of night.

Sometimes I Wake

Sometimes I wake in the very crux of night
Unbreathing, to gasp, as if the succubus
Of dread lay with me, my pillow damp, and rise,
Still panting air, and from the rage of sleep
Lurch to my feet, abandoning the tumbled sheets,
To stumble and wonder what it is that I have lost
In this thicket of dreams.

She of obligation parcels out
My days and bids me toil in vineyards of right:
Example, friend and father, provider
And protector of my flock, and I submit.
But where is the passion of my younger days?
Not of the flesh, but of the mind, to which
New things were utter sensuality.
O I could drink a book of rhymes and eat
The tales of Roland and Haroon; if hungry
Read a catalog of classes and conjure up
Confections of Kant or Kierkegaard
Or feasts of lattice theories, quantum's gauge.
And what of the aching longing to create?
To reach into chaos's eyes and make
A thing of blinding beauty?

Ron Searls

It's madness now or was or is and yet,
Though I tremble in the dark and think that all
Is past me, I sneak to the door and out onto
My porch and winter's bitter, final chill—
And into silence and a lambent moon,
And softly glow-lit trees, and all around
The pointile stars, nebulae, worlds, voids,
Galaxies, great attractors, blackest holes—
Infinities on infinities on—and I relearn:
It yet awaits and I will yet return.

Evening Sonnet

When I look on this all encroaching night,
That even high summer's eves cannot delay,
I think on sweet gone hours, on mornings bright,
When children's questions crowed the break of day,
I muse on vows exchanged under noon's blue dome,
Paths walked in shadows amid the forest green,
What draws a driftless wanderer from wild to home,
Like a bee at day's end to buzzing hive and queen.
My sun lays now her red hair on brown hill,
Her drowsy eyes half see the yellow moon,
The universe will all its secrets spill
To her last upward gaze in darkness soon—
And as we fall beneath the edge of sleep
We dream of love at midnight, dark and deep.

The Empty Room

She is gone now, but all remains:
Her lipstick, red sword ensheathed,
A scarf, yet scented with citrus,
Lounges over the back of her chair
Above the cat she loves beneath,
The ticket stubs from our plays
And our symphonies and our movies,
Their ragged edges half-aligned,
Sleep in a celandine bowl
Like tired siblings after trips to the sea.

Sunlit afternoon strikes an open book—
The poetry she writes is mysterious,
Like "Kublai Khan"—left exposed beneath
The judgmental library around,
Shakespeare, Milton, Wordsworth,
All peering down with slitted eyes.
When at our keyboard, with hands arrayed,
She plays the piano like Chopin played,
I am so moved, then see the photographs:
She, her mother, our daughter,
The three in one,
And the time we stayed in Erice
In the castle in the clouds
And I saw, in lamplight, wearing

Clouds like silk, in the twilight,
Her.

But now she may not return to you,
My empty room—you into quantum change,
Superposition become, of life and death—
You hold the last evidences of her,
The shadow of her existential sun,
Left to haunt or fade, or, are but a next stage
On the ways of her, waiting to be rearranged,
The promise she will come back—
At the door now, about to knock,
Surely, or . . . the doctors will call.
I am only here, for her things,
Then will return to the ICU
And hold her trembling hand.

On Her Cancer

She is Joan. On that last day, morning's
Damp shadows still clog the streets, as the cart
Of weathered gray wood slips, jerks,
Gravid wheeling its sobbing way through
The corridor of English pikes, under dumb
Whitewashed walls in black timbers cased,
And twisted glass, reflecting futile heavens.
From the prison to the market square she rides.
Now dismounted, her soundless, shuffling feet,
Forced to obey, cross cold cobbled stones, as her
Dark eyes beseech the heartless eyes of Rouen.
Then glances up, she, stricken by the pyre
That the cruel *godons* have built high,
And the death she dreads trembles her, the fire.
Joan is she.

She is Joan. The clinic, the cathedral, on
Her right, Saint-Sauveur, looms. Her hair
Is shorn, cropped close; she wears the same shift,
They all do. Her confession, her blood, is drawn.
Her recent scars are red, on belly and breast,
The arrow at Orleans for the reconstruction,
The crossbow at Paris, the mastectomy.
It is not the treacherous Winchester or Cauchon
Pronouncing judgment, from the double stands

Under the buttresses, but her doctors four,
In their gowns like robes, general surgeon,
Plastic surgeon, oncologist, radiation
Oncologist, in careful voices:
"Heretic"—it is ductal carcinoma,
"Relapsed"—the cancer is invasive,
"Apostate"—the cancer is multi-focal,
"Idolater"—the cancer is in the nodes.
Joan is she.

She is Joan. Though I step with her to the pyre,
Stumble on the splintered oak and give
My last encouragement, a cross to hold
To her tortured breast, and whisper my absolutions
Of recovery, I must step down. She is alone,
Strapped to her stake, the IV tree, the drip.
The executioner fans the coals, the heat
Crawls on our faces, the nurse brings the vials
Of "A:" Adriamycin, red-devil, Drano.
Thick gloves protect this nurse, like the hood
The executioner. Is his voice just as soft?
She handles the tubes, injecting the poison, which
Red snakes into the vein, eager, even
As the flames take and gray smoke rises,
Writhes, obscures, but cannot mute the screams.
Joan is she.

She is Joan. Her immune system,
Her armor, by the Burgundians at
Compiègne, is stripped away, the helmet first

Then guantlets, arms, pauldrons, breastplate and back,
Then legs, then feet, so that she suffers sores
And abscesses, and cannot sleep. No appetite
Has she. Her jailers keep her awake, taunt
With threats of rape. They show her the instruments
Of torture, the screws, and for the fire, irons
And spikes. But only show. Her fatigue won't end.
She cannot escape. Nightmares often come:
I do not love her—Charles will not ransom pay—
I will leave her—France will be undone—
The voices are not the saints, but devil's tears.
Joan, Joan, Joan—Joan is she.

She is Joan. And when this desolation
Of the body, this loss of parts, this struggle, this
Indignity, this trial that was not sought,
This curse of self, this invitation of death,
This called down destruction, this napalm on
The soul, lays waste, burns through to bones,
It's her passion that remains, my heart enthralls.
O Joan, not maiden, sweetheart, braveheart mine
Come home and we will thrive! I've flowers, I've wine,
I've all the dreams. I'll make you breads and tea
And pile up pillows. Creation songs I'll sing
Like Orpheus, and harrow hell. Look to me,
To me, your Margaret, Catherine, Michael
I will be! Take me with you Joan, O Joan,
O Joan how can you leave?

Bonebreaker

He's the blackness of the asphalt, the goth of every turn,
The prowler in ruined buildings, crouched in rusted steel.
He skulks in dim lit alleys, where darkness ruts and breeds.
He lurks in echoing tunnels, in pale litter and dank weeds,

And when I cannot see him, only then begin I to breathe.
And when guitars of evening, cry upon the breeze,
And talk of life is easy and friends are close and free,
And love begins its stirring, I forget that he is he.

But when the sun wakes up, when the road again is long,
My lidded eyes start scanning, for him, the waiting one.
He is the prince of shadow, the magister of fear,
The unquiet of apprehension, the disquiet of a leer.

I've taken roads that wander, and walked for mile on mile,
Been lost in a song's creation or chased a sudden smile
Or traveled to the sounding sea and in its lulling rhyme,
Fallen into star cropped dreams that cull me out of time,

Only to rise and pace and pace and pace that one paved way,
As I become automaton just shuffling to its grave.
My anxiety unbidden cries: forebode, forebode, forebode.
I cannot escape, we'll meet, at a winding in the road,

Where then it might be nothing, or a racking of the mind,
Downbeats of the song eternal, white novas of the soul,
Or poetry itself on fire—but always the dark must fall,
The road dissolve into wildness:—then no more turns at all.

The Winter of Life

When the winter of life began
I went out into the coldest night,
I asked the swirling stars to hold,
The ascendant moon to halt in place,
I bid wild rivers cease to flow,
The wind into feckless eddies sink.
I saw a great horned owl
And looked it in its golden lens
And begged it end its clockwork scans.
I asked the wolf to stop its howl
And the bear no more to wake.

When all of roiling nature stopped
In bated silence, deep and still,
I became the great eye of the world
With the leisure at last to view
The symmetry of each snowflake,
The bend of limb and tree, to map
The figures and fissures of the sky
Of paralyzed stars, spread out above,
Held motionless in place for me,
As encaged midnight, anxious, paced.

Freed from the crabbed hands of time,
The things that I had loved, the words,

The faces, pouts and sighs, cool
Touches yet that burned, yearnings,
Despairs, images, songs, tastes,
Flew at me and I caught them up
Into a window of stained glass
Connected by my leaded bones
And lit by memory's pale fire—
Creation is metamorphosis.

I stood upon a dark, dark shore
Above a sea of chaos without end,
Immersed in a solitary music that
The universe like a cello played,
The birth canticle of forever,
Whose chords, curtains of auroras,
Entangled the night and drew me up,
Till I fell back into the march of hours,
Rapt in its song. I did not grieve
When morning and its requiem came.

Autumn Interrupted

Deep in the night—now Autumn is foreclosed
By early snows; from thick sleep, he escapes,
Across black stubble fields stiff stumbles, deposed;
Slow dropping rime a white cloak round him drapes.

He flees past barn and silo, through garden gate,
Where unseasonable roses bend to greet,
And recalls the smile of Summer that so late
Had kept the willow green and orchard sweet.

It should not be this way when Summer strays,
He thinks, and sighs out frosty, smoky clouds,
She'd swirled her colored skirts with red, red rays
And promised illicit joy in emerald shrouds.

She'd lingered past the equinox, she'd skyed
Her chartreuse dreams, still clinging to her trees,
Wild leaves, in dissolution's riot died,
As Summer's dress was furled by sudden freeze.

And on it came, that gargoyled ogre cold,
Pushed ripening, yearning limbs aside and took
The heat of Summer, and all that fairy gold
Of pumpkins, apples and corn from every nook.

This time the Old One stayed for but a night—
And they woke once more, restored, to simmering sun;
He chased her through glades of flickering leaves and light
And forgot again the thing that yet must come.

A German Requiem (1968)

for Saud

We flew that summer like two careless crows
Surveying that resurrected Fatherland.
In Sindelfingen, while I awaited you,
I walked in graveyards looking for remorse;
I walked in green forests of throttled pines;
I walked in precise rows of yellow tasselled corn;
I pondered existential works and Keats's poems
And longed for the woman with brown eyes.
In Nuremberg I found an ancient book
And all around things barely understood
Seemed pregnant with a higher meaning:
All things were possible when you arrived.

In Erlangen, I drank the late wine, chilled, gold,
And you began to tell stories which did not have
An end, I don't recall if they even began before
I was transported, so eager was I for heaven.
We drove the Mercedes down narrow streets,
Amid crowds of gnomes and trolls and good
Germans in leather pants and blond women
Who people had died for, wearing blouses with
Flowers stitched around tiny eyelets lined in
Blue thread. It was all correct. I could not recall
The children, at least then. There must have been . . .

Wordsworth for hours we read around Augsburg
As we drove. On the longest evening we saw fires
On the hills, purposeful, contained. Who burned
In these fires? Were they holocausts? Was some
Latter-day pagan consumed there to placate a spirit
Who now no one could comprehend? Or was it
Far worse? But it was St. John's Eve I learned
Later. So those might have been new saints
Cooking on the hills or watch-fires for armies
Sanctified by priests, waiting to arise, once again
Clamoring for the east—or just dead wood.

We met the weird sisters in Bamberg, the fates.
One was betrothed to a Marine, Saigon bound.
I tried to discern my own future in her eyes
As we walked over the graves of notables,
As we walked by the cathedral buttresses
That hands had taken a hundred years to place,
Which now warmed us with retained heat.
I envied the stone its certitude, its fitness—
But it will have fallen, eventually, though it
Stand for unnumberable years. The bomb damage
Had all been erased, and the suffering, which
We all knew was deserved, could be ignored.

We drove into the country then, on roads unmarked.
We walked in meadows where moving suns
Wrote messages in the milkweed script,
Published by the wind, in which we read
Indescribable tales. From you I learned about all of

Them, the writers, your friends, before there
Were Germans: Novalis, Tieck, Wackenroder,
Hoffmann, Kleist. We read Faust in several
Languages and "Eine Reise nach Prague."
If we found a piano, you would play. And I would
Think of Chopin, who didn't belong here,
And Beethoven, who did.

We saw cities, like clippers, tacking on the plain,
With spires and minarets and campaniles,
And princeless towers where silent ladies mourned,
Thickets of brambles, barriers of pointed thorns,
Orchards of blue flowers in blue haze,
Knights who searched the morning land
For treasures that could not be transcribed,
Whole armies that disappeared into the south,
Crusaders with fleshless cheeks with crosses colored
With the blood of Semites, sacrificed for lost
Reasons, reconquistas or for Jerusalem's estate.

From deep green woods we often heard tales
Of changeless women and deformed men,
Of enchanted woods where time was stopped.
Entire forests could be found in one small valley;
If you had lifetimes they could not be crossed
Though they did not span one mile. We spoke
With woodcutters and dwarves and searched
For mushrooms and came upon sudden houses
With woven umber roofs with brooms outside
A solitary door and old women who might

Have been beautiful or under a spell, who might
Have full red lips, if we could only kiss them.

We saw eagles hunting the heights
Even as they had when legions marched,
Bearing Rome's gifts which had first to be bought
With the blood, bones of broken cracked men,
Tribes of Teutons chewed to the marrow
By the implacable engines of Caesar.
What had they made of the straight-walled forts,
The ballistas, the uniform, the precision that
Marshalled small courage into a wall of points
That not even Wotan dared to cross? Gods
Undone by right-angles, woods by whetstones,
Passion by undecorated, calculated thought.

We crossed a treeless border into Austria.
As the Gross Glockner wept winter's ice
Above, we stopped at the child's memorial,
As I had stopped in the heart of Reichmannsdorf,
Reading of death in the east, and in the west
And even near us there were rumors of dead men,
Ghosts of millions wandering in the lost fields
Of succorless wheat, which beckoned as if
Searching for dead gods which were not myths.
You translated the inscription so carefully hung
In that tiny chapel of wood, now weathered,
Which, through how many winters and summers
Had stood, we knew not, and wondered
How she had to be so remembered.

And we knew that death was overcome by a love
Which lingered long in the deaf, indifferent hills.
We drank then from the stream, tumbling, clear,
Because it was consecrated, sweet, holy.

In the mountains I witnessed a thunderstorm at night.
As blue bolts networked cloud erupting skies,
I saw visions of other heavens, alien worlds
Where whole races of men consumed
Themselves, with dumb hatred raining red
Death upon their own children, homes wrecked
With bright beams, ancient works of art
Sacrificed, complete histories erased.
While cool brother against brother contrived
Murder for the sake of strange symbols, entire
Pantheons of gods wept in black despair
At evil that defied even pointlessness,
As they fled their creatures, forever,
Their eon crossing steps, miles, miles
And miles for miles echoed even as clots
Of white anger exploded in front of my eyes.

Two months I remained, coffee in the morning,
Often with speck, warm bread at lunch and cheese,
In the evenings the beer and *gulas suppe*. I
Heard stories from the soldiers, the *Nahkämpfers*,
The ones who had left only fingers in Russia.
But everywhere there was a great silence, between
Careful breaths, between the words, between
And even around the voices of the children,

These pale children of Mozart, Goethe, Bach,
A great silence rolling always down
From the sky, from the mountains down, hovering, in voids
Whispered, waning, wanting, wavering, weeping,
Symphonies, songs, sonnets, stories, speech,
Lost, lost, lost, receding, that, now,
Never will have been, been made, said, sung.
I knew then of death, loss that outlasted stone;
I knew then abysses more muted, utter, deep,
Than love could cross or imagination leap.

Café Budapest

Come winter, come blood slogging chill,
Come flayer of branches, contortionist of ice,
Come in wan evenings and wreathing fogs,
Come in neon moons and shrouds of white,
In long gray shadows and low orange suns,
In dragster blizzards, spinning wheels of snow
Into fountains of mists and green lightning, come.
Strike down from contrails scratched above
With chalk-sticks of hoar and frozen light.
Come panting in sidled smokestack's breath
And beg with rag-wrapped hands held out
And shiver in cardboard atop a sidewalk grate
While the dead in stasis stack up above iron grounds.

In the thrall of winter the censers cannot burn,
The sacrificial kindling quick damps out,
Stuttered prayers struggle to scale deaf heavens.
But laughter in the lowering cold, mortal music,
Encircles the guests in the haven of a basement café,
This icon of lost Budapest reborn in the warmth
Of Helena, Edith, Hedda, mother and daughters.
They escaped the dire wolves on left and right,
The dripping yellow fangs, the carrion breath
And swollen tongues of hate and growling war,
To abide with us. Those three were our new Fates,

We measured and cut the threads of our lives by them:
The remembrances of banns and births, love's chase
And well met friends, the days of saints and ember.

Through St. Stephen's arms on rampant doors
Down we stepped, even on the most bitter nights,
Down the steps of red into other worlds
Done up with walls of silk and green brocades,
Silvered vitrines with Herend figurines inset,
Cocktails waiting, glimmering at the marble bar
And cognac and the lady in white whose lowered glove
Reveals the number on her arm and the violins
Alive with glissandos of gypsy whirl and dance,
Confabulations of Liszt, Schubert and Strauss,
As the formal waiters served the cherry broth,
Gulyas, paprikash and the wines of Tokay:
A sanctuary of the senses raised against the chaos
Of the gelid, gathering dark. But what is this?

The cross is gone from that door on Exeter Street,
Gone are they all. The last of them has died.
Our modern gods are mortal; the steps are shut
Against us, beauty at auctions sold, now years
Ago. Soon, those who pass will know
No longer what within these rooms once lived,
As they bundle coats closer and angle heads
Into the effacing winds of snow and cutting ice,
As the harbor clogs and skaters slice across
The stiffened uncrackable surface of the Charles.

Then come winter, brutal as your hands are,
And though you bully time, and our lives cull,
You are not the end of anything, or law.
New gods await. The revolving earth will thaw.

Half Life

You're gone... the call just... but dead?
Yet we just spoke together: you recalled
The Italian trip and I the cemetery in Rome,
You Shelley's grave and Keats, I
The Spanish Steps and you the room and I
The fireplace where Severn cooked for him.
We both remembered the beach at Viareggio,
Wondering where Shelley's body rose
And what those poets said around the pyre.
I reminded you how bright his house was
In Lirice in July and the flowers at noon,
And you, me, Portonevere and lunch,
How the fish were fried whole and the sweet wine
Of Cinque Terre and how the sun had set
On the Gulf of Poets.

We've met so rarely since, but when we do,
Words from my last imagined sentence leap
From you. You can't be gone! I refuse...
This knowledge poured into my ear kills
What lived, what in imagination thrived.
Mere words. Mere bits. Why not ignore? Deny?
You were only just alive. I—I can't
Abstract. But only remember you? What good's
It to be an internal thing, a puppet jerked

If I enact? Before this rumor you at least
Half-breathed, half-ate, half-slept. The possible's
Forsaken my unraveled thoughts...and you've died twice.

I visions like cathedrals build where we
Two speak as you do live. Now false, this one
At last, its stained glass shattered, bells unrung,
Turns to an arched thing of gargoyled gloom,
Of chantless choirs, requiems unsung,
Of hymnals stacked on pews, of vows unvoiced,
Of pulpits where earless lamentations rise:
I would have soaked up the sweat upon your brow
Or held you, though seizures wracked, or read some lines
From "Tintern Abbey," moaned with you as you moaned
Through the tensed hours of leaving that grind the soul.

Then gone. Then are we ever not apart?
A year, a day, an hour—what difference made
If Memory, barren goddess, cold, cannot
Beyond the instant when we look away
Remake a living hand. How then do we know?
Come back! Yes, (I grab you)—touch—it must
Be that. Or your voice: keep speaking, tell me tales!
Or your dark eyes that shone—Or the bread we broke—
Or the shared cigarettes. The senses fed the mind.
That's how we transpired, I think too late.
We grasp so little in that lived moment.

Your body's vapor, mine is ached and bent,
There's no more concurrent hour for us,

These eyes, your eyes, will no more comprehend.
And now though I'd power over all of sense,
Could paint the red on memory's ashen cheek,
Hang shanks on a vision's bones, a thumping heart
Place in desire's breast, give it your voice,
Thoughts, rhymes, songs—it would be what
You were, not are, immutable, stopped, fixed,
A clockwork thing, the past's automaton.
The work unfinished, that is who we are.

The mind can not vault its own abyss,
It needs one quantum of the other, real:
A single photon can daybreak an alien sky;
A universe on this one thing it hangs,
Realms of gods and untold reachless space,
Love, passion, the sacrifice of self.
But that bit gone, my dream of you abrades.
Your face is now in shadow, hushed voice low.
A chair scrapes—feet scuff—you turn
At the edge of darkness—stop—one final gaze . . .
But I cannot see your eyes. Then go.

Then go! Return to that wild mystery
That haunts the edge of what we almost know,
That teases out perfection, taunts desire.
Return, but do not fade! Become the wind,
The storm, the clouds piled high, the thunderclap—
Lightning scrabbling down the stratosphere,
A star ripped through unexpurgated night,
For then I'll startle as a newborn does,

Surprised by life beyond its lethal eyes,
And know, though halved, that we, cross death's divide
Entangled, touch: that I, as you, abide.

Le Tombeau de Faisal

Sing lute, of clove-scented winds that hiss and roar
Round Uhud Mountain's shoulders, then sing of the way
White stallions, down dunes, like an avalanche spray,
Carrying black riders to distant thunderheads of war.

Sing of the falcons that scrape the sky and soar—
Then, like arrows, fall, in ringing dives, to the curlew prey.
Sing of abandoned campfires, black tents now swept away
And sing, my lute, that he—that Faisal is no more.

Song from silence arises, in its first notes it seeks
The bazaar of sensuality, a *baharat* of tastes and smells,
And in kohl lined eyes, in henna'd skin—lusts to transcend.

"But beauty is beyond," the desert night yet speaks.
Sing oud! Sing ney! to its infinite stars, its lonely gazelles—
At sunrise we'll then know:—all great songs must end.

Elegy for John B___

The count begins at eight hundred.

You stood upon my December porch,
It seems but three years ago.
The sun was bright with morning;
Camellias white and crimson gleamed;
Upon our door lay a wreathe you wove.
In top hat, morning suit, tails,
You could have stepped from a page of Dickens
As you met each guest with a carol clear.
O angel tenor, how you loved the song!
But I cannot hear it.
Is it cold time which battens up my ear?
Or do I only listen for the ghost
Of my own Christmas, my past?

The count is now six hundred.

Two summers ago, you dwelled with us,
My three children and my gardens
were your care—all thrived
within your hands—it was a time
of violets, of water and of glee.
My son remembers how together
you two worked the plants in that

garden which is gone.
We spoke of holly, azaleas, jade,
Phlox, ferns—I recall the
meal you made even for me.
But I was wary, and like some
secret vampire, squinted for
signs of blood.
They did not know.

The count is now four hundred.

I saw you that last time, only a year ago,
As you worked once more, the garden.
I watched you with hidden eyes, peeking
from behind eyelids of guilt
Upon your wizening frame, as the sweat
Sheened your skin, as you gleaned
In the afternoon.
I noticed: as you moved,
Your muscles moved too clearly;
You were like some northern god
Whose magic armor had been tricked away
By a scheme of Loki;
You stood naked on a planet I dared not reach,
Etched by alien fire.
How could we both be on this one earth?

The count is now two hundred.

In the evening gloom I look

Out to the lamp post, by the water-oak.
You dressed it in jasmine, which only
Now has bloomed, belated gift,
So sweet, the florets pressed to my face
Summon dreams of Arabian nights—antique perfumes—
I breathe for you.

O that I were a Prospero, and my Ariel art
Command the raging tempest of disease
To speed you to an isle as full of song and sweet,
Forever, as this moment that you grew for me.
But my futile numbers cannot awake:
You sleep in the coma god's arms,
Protected with implacable grace.

The count is zero.

Moonbeams alone alight—
I hear you son, my brother, my love:
The whip-poor-will
Voices requiem in the thickets of the night;
The funeral owl is your spirit's flight;
Away it lofts, drifts, soars,
Leaves:—
This earthen, leaden, clotted heart,
Which longs, O, which longs,
For my lost, my John of flowers,
My forlorn, my John of songs.

Author's Note: John was a florist and had a beautiful tenor voice. He died from complications of AIDS when he was only twenty-six. Before he was too disabled to work, my wife and I hired him to look after our children and gardens. The "count" in the poem is John's T-cell count.

Mnemosyne

She brought him home, that great wreck of a man,
Who used to pilot those bright ships that streamed
Across the blue. He no longer can
Carry us to the places we once dreamed
About. He was a giant then to our
Small eyes, brought us impala hides and masks
From the Congo and the Amazon. But now
The doctors tell us that his memory's power
Is wasting, Alzheimer's they guess, and all the tasks
Of mind we take for given, knot up his brow.

She loves him still, though every day it drains
Her. She sets the clock, turns the calendar page,
Reminds him, though there's nothing he retains,
What he did yesterday. Her, his eyes engage
When someone asks him something he's forgot,
And then she answers. When we children come
She smiles in our direction, her eyes alight,
We're from the deepest past, which he has not
Yet lost; a while a family we become,
And then she holds his hand into the night.

Her skin is thin as paper, moon white pale,
Blue veins in rivers complicate her arms.
The hands with which she feeds him herself ail,

But still she can depend upon those charms
That once beguiled Zeus, to bend him to
Some small purpose. But she cannot restore
The days which from his wintering mind now drop
Like leaves in autumn, joys lost beyond review.
Though she smiles yet and speaks of times before,
Not even a titaness can dissolution stop.

She is the force that binds. The very things
Themselves that all around us lie, the stones
Beneath our feet, the familiar face which brings
Us pleasure, songs the songbirds voice, the tones
Of bells that brazen out the morn, would all
Vanish, to us be unperceived as air
Without her touch. Change is not change unless
We remember. But still she frets, a tall
Shade moving in dark rooms, taking care
To line up his pants and shoes so he can dress.

He has escaped her. He's on a rocket ride
To an inward earth, ours now falls behind.
Already in the second stage, he looks inside
As we recede, to her bosom we're confined.
He lives in weeks, and soon it will be days,
Then hours, minutes, seconds—until time dies.
Into the eternal now he will burst through,
Into a swirl of colors, streaks. He'll gaze
On alien landscapes that we cannot surmise,
Where nothing changes, but all is always new.

   . . . Goodbye rocketman, father, adieu.

Rite

I washed her body down, afterwards,
I did not feel the air
Or the coldness of the room
My body become monument
A thing without a breath.
I caressed her eyelids shut,
First the right, then the left,
But maybe the other way.
I wiped the still soft lips
That were so often kissed.
I put gold earrings on her
And the necklace round her
Neck, which no longer pulsed,
And as I laved her with the oil
I questioned the other drops
That fell to her ribs:
Love cannot end, can it?
It must outlast.
I thought I heard a requiem...
Denn alles fleisch, es ist wie grass...
As I dressed her in a kimono
I had split. The last vision
That cannot last, the end
That must be ended...
And I must leave at last,

Must—must—but—
How does a stone move itself?
Or memory forget?
I washed her body down.

Midnight Sonnet

When all the shining moments of my years,
Against the others' dullness are arrayed,
They are as stars above my midnight fears,
As dreamless, I twist, and think that all will fade.
Arching constellations, transcendent forms,
Things of the past which time's deep fathoms cross,
I see around me: hot love's solar storms,
Supernovas of ecstasy, black holes of loss.
But beauty calls to beauty, though this night
Grind what remains, new stars must yet arise—
From the East, they slowly swirl into my sight,
What new patterns now I see, oh what surprise.
Though I depart, I leave above for you,
This star, these words, amid the indigo and blue.

Acknowledgments

"The Unmerged Star" (earlier revision as "Star Sonnet"), "Aubade" (earlier revision, as "Dawn Sonnet"), "Lament," "Lethe" (earlier revision), "To Devin," "The Puppet," "Elegy for John B____," "Summer's End," "Ode to the Internet" (earlier revision, as "Song of the Internet"), "Meditations on Chopin's Nocturnes," "Sometimes I Wake," "Evening Song," "On Her Cancer," "Half Life," "A German Requiem (1968)," "Mnemosyne," "In the Tombs," "Café Budapest" (earlier revision), "To a Glass Mercury," "Mauna Kea" (earlier revision), "The Death of Leviathan" (earlier revision), and "Autumn Interrupted" were privately published in *Distant Strains*, Second Edition, by Al-Sowayel, Saud and Searls, Ronald C., Bronxville: ISA Press, 2009.

"Mnemosyne" and "Songbird" were published in *The Lyric Magazine*, Vol. 97, Number 3, Summer 2017.

"Autumn Interrupted" was published in *The Lyric Magazine*, Vol. 98, Number 4, Autumn 2018.

"Elegy for John B____" was published in Indolent Books' online project "HIV Here and Now" on November 23, 2017.

"On Poetry" was published by *Verse Virtual*, an online journal, in April of 2018.

About the Cover

The tree in bloom on the cover is an American Chestnut, a tree that grew in my neighborhood in North Andover, Massachusetts. It is a tree for poetry: beautiful in bloom, magnificent in size, its fruit nourishing, its heartwood almost immortal, and its fate tragic.

Once spread throughout the Eastern United States, because of the chestnut blight introduced from Japan, it now exists like Sisyphus, fitfully growing from roots, only to be killed again and again. In 2004 I counted thirty trees, some thirty or forty feet tall, growing near me. They amazingly bloomed that year, and I was able to experience their beauty for myself. But the blight then killed every one of them, and I live on in the shadow cast by their memory.

About the Author

Ron Searls' poems have been published in *The Lyric Magazine*, *Verse Virtual*, and by Indolent Books' online project "HIV Here and Now." He is a recently retired software engineer. His last project was co-founder of Nanigans, Inc., an adtech startup. Before he retired, he remembered that he hadn't graduated from MIT, re-enrolled, and finished with the class of 2015.

www.ingramcontent.com/pod-product-compliance
Lightning Source LLC
Chambersburg PA
CBHW051347040426
42453CB00007B/453